Head teacher

C000110468

The National **Literacy** *Strategy*

Sentence Level Work

GREENMOUNT PRIMARY SCHOOL
LODGE LANE
BEESTON
LEEDS 11

Activity Resource Bank

Module 3

Oxford University Press

Department for Education and Employment

Oxford University Press, Great Clarendon Street, Oxford OX2 6DP

Oxford New York
Athens Auckland Bangkok Bogota Buenos Aires Calcutta
Cape Town Chennai Dar es Salaam Delhi Florence Hong Kong Istanbul
Karachi Kuala Lumpur Madrid Melbourne Mexico City Mumbai
Nairobi Paris São Paulo Singapore Taipei Tokyo Toronto Warsaw

and associated companies in Berlin Ibadan

Oxford is a registered trade mark at Oxford University Press

Individual pages of this book may be reproduced by individual teachers for class use
within the purchaser's institution. The material remains copyright under the Copyright,
Designs and Patents Act, 1998, or in the case of reprographic reproduction in
accordance with the terms of the licences issued by the Copyright Licensing Agency.

© Crown copyright 1998
Produced by Oxford University Press 1998
First published 1998

ISBN 0 19 918954 4

Typeset and designed by Ray Barker, Glen Franklin, Catherine Miller of the
National Literacy Association
Printed in Great Britain

© Crown copyright 1998

National Literacy Strategy Activity Resource Bank: Sentence Level at KS2

The following resource sheets provide a bank of suggestions for Sentence Level work at Key Stage 2 and include the sample sheets from the National Literacy Strategy Training Pack. They cover a selection of termly objectives. They are not complete 'Literacy Hours' because they focus on Sentence level only, although some activities do refer to opportunities for Text level work. Some sheets contain a list of resource suggestions as well. They are simply examples of books that teachers have found useful, or stories and poems that children have enjoyed and which illustrate the objective in an accessible way. **This is in no way prescriptive.** What matters are the outcomes.

Childrens' understanding of grammar is used in the early stages of reading as a way of checking if what has been read makes good sense, and to predict unfamiliar words. Early on, this process is intuitive and reflects the pattern of the child's everyday speech. When writing, children begin to imitate the grammatical structures used in different texts, to refine their understanding of what makes a sentence and how to use punctuation. By the time children leave Key Stage 1, most have gained a sufficient grasp of grammar to be able to read and write simple texts.

However, at this stage much of their knowledge is implicit. During Key Stage 2, children need to reflect explicitly and critically on the grammatical structures of different texts to improve their reading and writing, e.g. the more that children are able to use connectives such as *nevertheless, however, whereas, because,* the more they can argue persuasively a complex viewpoint. Without an understanding of how punctuation helps the reader, or the grammatical knowledge to order sentences, children cannot write or communicate their thinking effectively. Indeed, without the basic tools of sentence structure and the ability to manipulate language, thinking itself may be restricted.

Children need to know how word order affects meaning, the function of different words within sentences, how sentences can be extended and connected in different ways or trimmed for impact. They should know that some words are essential to meaning whilst others add variety and colour. If children are to improve their writing, they need to have control over the choices that lie open to them and to be able to consider critically what has been written in order to improve it. This needs a strong grounding in words, sentences and their functions in relation to different audiences and purposes. This work is taught to ensure that children are able to use Standard English effectively.

Children need to be taught to read as writers. They should listen to, identify and discuss critically how effects are gained, passages and sentences structured and words or phrases combined. Teaching should draw childrens' attention to grammatical features through Shared Reading and Writing. In Shared Writing, possible grammatical constructions and combinations should be modeled and explored. Children should be shown how to use this knowledge in their writing.

Grammar and punctuation are essential tools to help children revise and proof read work so that it is appropriate, effective and accurate. They play a central role in raising standards in childrens' writing while deepening their understanding and appreciation of reading. To do all of the above, children need to have acquired and refined basic grammatical concepts, to use grammatical terminology confidently and to apply this in their reading and writing. In geography, we use the term *erosion* and would not dream of talking about 'when the water rubs away the river bank'. So, too, in teaching English, we need to use specific vocabulary so that we can discuss the subtleties of language.

It is insufficient to believe that knowing different word classes or parts of speech on their own is satisfactory. The teaching of grammar is effective when children are taught to apply their knowledge to improve their reading and writing. It is essential to use the first part of the Literacy Hour to draw childrens' attention to grammatical features in their reading and to model grammatical use in Shared Writing. This should be built upon in the main part of the hour when activities are planned for children to practise, refine and use their knowledge. As different aspects of grammar work are introduced, they should be taught through reading and writing, and returned to on many occasions, so that childrens' understanding and use of ideas is refined over time. Without genuine opportunities to write for different audiences and to read each other's writing, the real need for revision, accuracy and using grammar appropriately is lost. The more pupils are taught to read as writers and to apply their knowledge to their own writing, the more their writing will improve.

Our thanks to Widgit Software for permission to use © graphics from their *Writing With Symbols* software package.

© Crown copyright 1998

NLS Activity Resource Sheet

Year	3
Term	1
Strand	S 1

Objectives

To use awareness of grammar to decipher new or unfamiliar words, e.g. to predict from text, read on, leave a gap and return; to use these strategies in conjunction with knowledge of phonemes, word recognition, graphic knowledge and context when reading.

Activities

N.B.
Support and teaching strategies:
Always aim at helping the reader towards independence. Rehearse strategies with the children, e.g. *Six things I can do if I get stuck before asking the teacher.* Make a chart of the strategies. Rehearse with them how much they know already.

Class
● Through Shared, Guided, Group and Independent Reading:

- mask out a word and keep going. Then go back and guess the word from context *(syntax and context)*
- go back to the beginning of a sentence and take a run at it - read back and read on *(syntax and context)*
- use initial and final sounds and blends *(phonics)*
- find words within words, compound words, etc.
- practise onset and rime: *If I know zip, I know blip, skip, ship (phonological knowledge, graphic knowledge)*
- investigate common letter clusters *(phonological knowledge, graphic knowledge)*
- make use of sight vocabulary from other sources: Where have I seen it? *(graphic knowledge - logographic)*
- use root words, prefixes, suffixes and inflections *(grammatical knowledge)*
- use picture information *(pictures - context).*

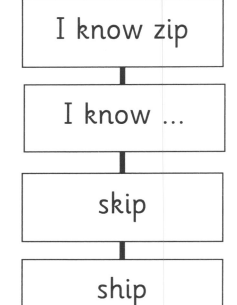

Group
● During Shared Reading, model strategies, e.g. masking words, cloze procedure and re-assembling cut-up sentences or words on cards.
● Provide wall charts, e.g. simple flow charts, or some prompt cards for children to keep in their reading diaries, to cover a range of procedures that help readers use cueing strategies.

Plenary
● Practise with a new shared text the strategies from the class chart.

Relevant published materials/resources

First Steps Reading Resource Book (Heinemann). **Independence in Reading,** Don Holdaway (Ashton Scholastic).

NLS Activity Resource Sheet

Year	3
Term	1
Strand	S 2

Objectives

To take account of the grammar and punctuation, e.g. sentences, speech marks, exclamation marks and commas to mark pauses, when reading aloud.

Activities

Class

● Through Shared, Guided, Group and Independent Reading:

- model a range of texts (plays, direct speech, narrative, non-narrative and pupils' writing, poetry, non-fiction);
- read in alternative ways and ask children to identify which is appropriate. See the Photocopiable Resource Sheets;
- ask children to read aloud and evaluate effectiveness;
- use Big Books to read a passage with one deliberate mistake, e.g. do not pause for a full stop;
- ask: How would this character say this?;
- use a text from which the punctuation has been removed, or masked out. Which punctuation fits best? Give the children a choice;
- practise choral reading, with the children making decisions as to how many voices there should be, intonation, dynamics and pace;
- read on to tape, stories or poems for other classes to use in listening corners;
- listen to tapes and follow the text, and imitate passages;
- read poems and performances of dialogues;
- prepare reading on own or with others of own writing.

How should this sound?

Which punctuation fits best?

How would this character say this?

Relevant published materials/resources

© Crown copyright 1998

NLS Activity Resource Sheet

Objectives

To understand the function of verbs in sentences through: collecting and classifying examples of verbs from reading and from own knowledge; experimenting with changing simple verbs in sentences and discussing their impact on meaning.

Activities

Shared or Group Reading

● Identify verbs, in sentences, as the words that contain action. Delete the verb and re-read to hear how the sentence does or does not work or loses power without the 'engine' of the verb. Circle verbs in a given text.

● Mask out or delete all the verbs in a Big Book to create a cloze procedure exercise. Let children consider alternatives and select the most appropriate verbs.

● Take out all the verbs in a text and insert nouns instead, e.g. *monkey*, to create an amusing variation of cloze procedure, e.g. *I monkeyed down the road.*

● Swop over verbs so that the wrong verb is in the wrong place; another variation of cloze procedure, e.g.

I plodded up this morning and woke down the stairs.

I ate as I yawned my breakfast.

● Make a verb alphabet, a verb for each letter, e.g. *act, buy, catch, dig, eat.*

● Select common verbs and list alternatives. Which group can list the most?

● Use colour coded words to consider the place and role of verbs in different sentences.

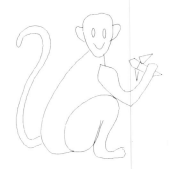

I monkeyed down the road.

Verbs of:

movement:
run, leap, bound, jump, hop
sound:
bang, crash, thump, sizzle
speech:
talk, whisper, chatter, shout
laughter:
laugh, giggle, snigger
cooking:
fry, boil, mash, bake, burn

Relevant published materials/resources

NLS Activity Resource Sheet

Year	3
Term	1
Strand	S 4

Objectives

To use verb tenses with increasing accuracy in speaking and writing, e.g.*catch/caught, see/saw, go/went*, etc. Use past tense consistently in narration.

Activities

N.B.
In the English language, it is the present and past tenses and participles which are identifiable by inflections *(is/was walking, had walked)*. Local dialect forms should not be denigrated but appropriate times for the use of spoken Standard English should be discussed and S.E. should be used in written English unless characters are given direct speech and need to use non-standard forms (see General Requirements for English, N.C.)

Class and Group

● In the context of a topic, a subject or an aspect of text, collect verbs to do with the subject. This is vocabulary extension and can form a spelling bank, e.g. sports verbs, *to ski, swim, run, jump, row,* etc. See the Photocopiable Resource Sheet.

● Practise by saying *I* and *s/he, you* (and names of others in class) with the verbs and in a sentence. Try all the possibilities and note the changes. Use real examples from the children, e.g. *I ran in the park yesterday; I went running in the park yesterday; we run in the park every day; Tracey runs in the park every day; I will run in the river tomorrow.*

● Read the text with incorrect verb or pronoun agreement. Ask the children to put you right.

Group

● Read the children's work or a prepared example aloud. Ask the children to identify where
   - past tense is incorrect, e.g. *I catched the ball;*
   - past and present tense are muddled;
   - incorrect grammatical agreement occurs, e.g. *we was late.*

● Let the children revise short passages or sentences with common errors that they are making.

● In Shared Writing, purposefully make an error then read specifically to check. Train the children to check for such errors in their own and their partner's work.

● Group those children who persist in such errors. List errors against the correct forms. Show the children how to check their work using such a list.

● Pro-actively mark work indicating errors and suggesting that children find and correct them, e.g. 'Find the two places where you have muddled we *was/were* and change them.'

Relevant published materials/resources

Oxford Junior Dictionary (OUP) – includes inflections and irregular forms, e.g. *run, runs, running, ran.* **Rosie's Walk**, Pat Hutchins (Puffin) or any text which has a simple list of events with a repeated syntactical pattern of past tense or where one can be added.

NLS Activity Resource Sheet

Year	3
Term	1
Strand	S 7

Objectives

To secure knowledge of question marks and exclamation marks in reading ... the basic conventions of speech punctuation.

Activities

N.B.
Speech marks relates to earlier work on the punctuation of speech.

Group

● Show where speech marks are used in texts. Explain their use. Many children will have some idea, some may even be using speech marks.

● Let the children investigate how speech marks are used and draw up a chart of rules, e.g. *We use speech marks when ..., You must remember to ...* . Use speech bubbles to isolate what is said from the rest of the narrative. Play *The animals spoke*. To do this, list zoo animals and each one speaks, e.g. The zebra said, "Let me keep my stripes." The lion roared, "Keep away from me."

● Provide examples of dialogue written on strips of paper. Ask children to match these with strips of paper containing narrative openings and endings for dialogue, e.g.

Tom said,	"Where are my custard pies?"
The king growled,	"I've not done my homework."
The clown whispered,	"Please pass me my crown."

● Children can invent dialogue and write onto strips of card. Others write possible narrative openings/endings. These can be pooled and matched to provide some amusing combinations.

● Give the children a passage to read with speech marks omitted. Children should proof read, beginning by circling what is actually spoken. Then they insert speech marks. Encourage use of dialogue in writing. Collect from reading different ways of setting out speech.

● Collect exclamations that teachers, parents and children make. List these. Show how they are set into dialogue. Children collect and list instances of exclamation marks in books they are reading. Make a chart to explain the use of exclamation marks.

● List exclamatory openings to stories, e.g. *Stop! Run for it! No way!* Practise saying these aloud.

● Give the children short extracts of dialogue, including some questions and some exclamations, for them to rehearse and then read aloud with expression.

Relevant published materials/resources

NLS Activity Resource Sheet

Year	3
Term	1
Strand	S 7, 8

Objectives

The basic conventions of speech punctuation through: identifying speech marks in reading; begin to use in writing; using capital letters to mark the start of direct speech. To use the term 'speech marks'.

Activities

Group

● The children chart how to set out dialogue when the speaker is mentioned before what is said, e.g. *John asked, "When is it time for tea?"* and after what is said, *"When is it time for tea?", asked John.* Produce this as a clear wall chart for children to use.

● The children collect and list as many ways as they can find to introduce or conclude dialogue, especially considering verbs instead of *said* and the use of adverbs. Discuss which sounds more effective, e.g. *she said quietly* or *she whispered.*

● Match and invent dialogue on strips of card to clauses where the speaker is mentioned before or after what is said.

Relevant published materials/resources

© Crown copyright 1998

NLS Activity Resource Sheet

Year	3
Term	1
Strand	S 9

Objectives

To notice and investigate a range of other devices for presenting texts, e.g. speech bubbles, enlarged or italicised print, captions and headings, inset text, etc. Explore purposes and collect examples.

Activities

Group

● The children use a range of texts to identify and list different features of print, layout and organisation. As these are discovered they can be added to an ongoing list. Beside each example give a suggested purpose:

- Use speech bubbles in cartoon form to separate what is said from the speaker.
- Rewrite a cartoon as narrative.
- Use enlarged prints for titles and headings in other work.
- Invent newspaper headings for events in fiction.
- Use headings in non-fiction. Practise writing headings neatly, so the letter size is even.
- Use captions in non-fiction to label drawings.
- Underline important words in text and list as a glossary with definitions.

Relevant published materials/resources

NLS Activity Resource Sheet

Year	3
Term	1
Strand	T 2

Objectives

How dialogue is presented in stories, e.g. through statements, questions, exclamations.

Activities

Class
- Identify different functions using a shared text and establish some basic distinctions.

Group
- The children look through books, or use a prepared text, to extract and list three examples of each, or discover which function is not common.
- Groups could seek examples of a selected function, e.g. one group lists questions while another looks for exclamations.
- In Shared Writing invent a character, e.g. a teacher or parent. List questions, exclamations, orders and statements that he or she might say.

How many times must I tell you?

Go and tidy your room!

Finished at last!

Relevant published materials/resources

NLS Activity Resource Sheet

Year	3
Term	1
Strand	T 11

To investigate and collect sentences/phrases for story openings and endings; use some of these formal elements in re-telling and writing.

Activities

N.B.
Most activities, once modelled during class Shared Reading and Word/Sentence Level Work, will be suitable for independent group work.
The value of many of these activities will be in collaborative work generating discussion of text structure, grammar, vocabulary etc. Non- fiction texts can also be usefully explored in this way.

Class

● Over time, investigate, categorise and list a class collection of openings and endings. Discuss what the introduction tells the reader, and whether it makes the reader want to read on. Discuss children's opinions about endings.
● Use the class collection of openings as a stimulus for shared and individual/group writing.

Group

● Use a spider diagram to tease out information provided in a story opening. See the Photocopiable Resource Sheet. This can be made into a game of *Find the Clues*.
● Stop reading before the end of a story or passage. Ask children to predict, orally or in writing, what the ending will be. Compare with the real ending and evaluate.
● Ask the children to collect text openings and endings on cards, from books in class for another group to match an opening with an ending. Retain these for future use.
● Provide a selection of cards with text openings, middle-extracts and endings for children to match up and classify.
● Provide a selection of cards with text openings for children to match with book covers and titles, characters and authors. See the Photocopiable Resource Sheet.
● Look in books and list favourite opening sentences. Categorise similar openings and imitate, e.g.

> Warnings: Tom's master told him not to play on the railway line ...
> Questions: "Where's papa going with that axe?"
> Exclamations: "Stop!"
> Names: Sally stared at her shoes; she was in trouble.

Relevant published materials/resources

Focus English: Reading Strategies at KS2, C. Buckton, P. Corbett and G. Mathews (Heinemann).

NLS Activity Resource Sheet

Year	3
Term	2
Strand	S 1

Objectives

To use awareness of grammar to decipher new or unfamiliar words.

Activities

N.B.
It is important that children who are not confident with their reading are assessed using a running record. This means that the area of cueing where they need support will be able to be best targeted.

Class
● Continue to remind the class of strategies using a text as a model, e.g. a newspaper story – with copies or on an OHP.

Group
● Make sense of text by using knowledge of syntax and context:

> - by re-reading and reading on;
> - by fine-tuning with phonemic and graphic knowledge;
> - by inferring meanings from clues from surrounding sentences, the whole sentence or theme of the passage;
> - by checking with a partner.

● Cloze procedure – discussing and making 'best guesses' based on all the information.
● Listening to each other reading, and helping to spot errors.
● Becoming used to 'listening' to one's own reading and spotting errors.
● Model monitoring own reading for sense and self-correction.

Relevant published materials/resources

NLS Activity Resource Sheet

Year	3
Term	2
Strand	S 2

Objectives

The function of adjectives within sentences, through identifying adjectives in Shared Reading; collecting and classifying adjectives, e.g. for colours, sizes, moods, etc.

Activities

N.B.
Relate this work to poetry or story writing.

Class
- In Shared Reading notice and identify adjectives.
- List the nouns and adjectives that might accompany them.
- Write webs of adjectives around a noun.

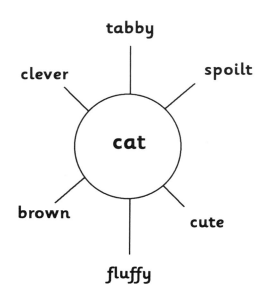

tabby
clever
spoilt
cat
brown
cute
fluffy

Group
- Collect unusual adjectives. The children could collect favourite adjectives in a word bank.
- Play adjective I Spy - *I Spy with my little eye something that is red ...* , etc.
- Which group can find and list the largest number of adjectives?
- List under headings, e.g. colours, sizes, moods, touch, taste, smell, sounds, shapes.
- Play *The headteacher's cat is a ... cat*, with an adjective for each letter of the alphabet.
- Use cloze procedure with adjectives omitted.
- Provide a passage with too many adjectives, three or four for each word. Discuss and trim.
- Ask children to underline, circle or highlight adjectives in poems or narrative.
- Encourage and model thoughtful and judicious use of adjectives in writing.
- Use colour coded words to help children understand the relationship between adjective and noun, their place in a sentence and to see how they can be removed and the basic sense of the sentence retained.

Relevant published materials/resources

NLS Activity Resource Sheet

Year	3
Term	2
Strand	S 2

Objectives

The function of adjectives within sentences, through: identifying adjectives in Shared Reading; discussing and defining what they have in common; experimenting with deleting and substituting adjectives and noting effects on meaning.

Activities

Class or Group
- In Shared or Guided Reading, notice and collect well-chosen adjectives.
- Identify any adjectives that might not be needed, e.g. where they state the obvious, such as in 'the red letterbox', or 'the hot flame'.
- Pause while reading and suggest alternative adjectives.
- Prepare a cloze procedure, where the adjectives have been removed from a passage.

The red letterbox!

- In Shared or Group Writing, demonstrate by working on short pieces of writing, or several sentences, how to select adjectives. Try using lots of adjectives. Does this enhance the sentence or do they clash together? Is an adjective needed? Which one is most appropriate? Does the adjective say something special about the noun?
- Use colour-coded words to create sentences, highlighting nouns and adjectives in distinct colours.
- Create categories and classify adjectives.

Relevant published materials/resources

© Crown copyright 1998

NLS Activity Resource Sheet

Year	3
Term	2
Strand	S 4

Objectives

Understanding the term *collective noun* and collecting examples. Experiment with inventing other collective nouns.

Activities

N.B.
Link to Text level poetry work.

Class and Group

● Brainstorm, search texts and list collective nouns. Use dictionaries and word banks to find as many as possible. Create a group glossary of those found or list as a poem.

● Invent new collective nouns, e.g.

> a roll of pencils,
> a plumpness of puddings,
> a scattering of spiders,
> a splash of swimsuits,
> a relic of homework.

● Children will enjoy some of the more unusual collective nouns that are no longer in current use, e.g.

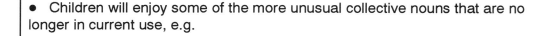

A parliament of owls

a plague of locusts

a school of whales

a gaggle of geese

a rope of pearls

a cluster of stars

Relevant published materials/resources

NLS Activity Resource Sheet

Year	3
Term	2
Strand	S 4

Objectives

To extend knowledge and understanding of pluralisation.

Activities

Class and Group

- Give the children prepared texts which they have to transform from singular to plural or plural to singular. Work in pairs, checking each other's work.
- Take sentences and discuss with the class the implications, discussing agreement, e.g.

> This girl is happy - These girls are happy.
> I am in the zoo - We are in the zoo.
> The farmer is eating - The farmers are eating.
> The boy likes a pudding - The boys like puddings, etc.

- Encourage the children to read their work aloud to hear if it 'sounds' right.
- List the effects of singular/plural on different verbs, e.g. to be:

They are   We are   She is   I am

He is   You are

- Investigate and collect words which cannot be pluralised, e.g. sheep.
- Practise and reinforce through cloze procedure exercises.
- Use a wall chart of common errors to help children proof-read their own work.

Relevant published materials/resources

NLS Activity Resource Sheet

Objectives

To extend knowledge and understanding of pluralisation.

Activities

Class or Group
- Play 'I spy' as a way of introducing the notion of nouns.
- Brainstorm and list nouns, naming objects in the classroom, outside, in a bedroom or kitchen, etc. Use labels if necessary. List nouns under different headings, e.g. cars, flowers, buildings, places, animals.
- List nouns in two columns, showing singular/plural.
- Circle, underline or highlight nouns in pieces of writing.
- Play 'I went to the shop and bought a ... and a ... and a ...', etc.
- List alphabets of nouns e.g. 'Things our caretaker found on the school roof': apple, ball, cat ...
- If the children are unsure, let them apply the 'pluralisation test' – if it is a noun there are usually singular and plural versions.
- Use colour coding to reinforce understanding nouns and their place in sentences.
- Let children give alternatives to common nouns, e.g.

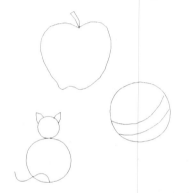

Things our caretaker found on the school roof

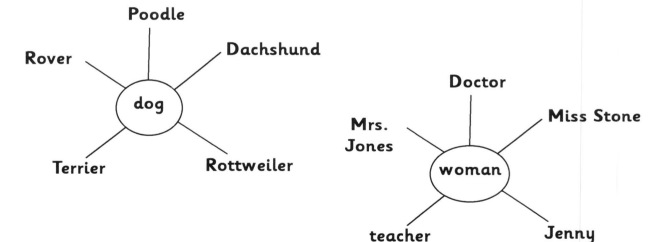

Relevant published materials/resources

NLS Activity Resource Sheet

Objectives

To extend knowledge and understanding of pluralisation. To use the terms *singular* and *plural* appropriately.

Activities

Group

● Collect from own spelling knowledge and from scanning texts a range of words spelled singular and plural. List these and begin to categorise into different types depending on what happens to the spelling of the plural, e.g.

> dwarf - dwarves
> church - churches
> child - children
> dog - dogs

● Encourage the children to generate rules for different categories but note common exceptions.
● Produce personal and class charts to remind the children and assist them when spelling.
● Use terms singular and plural in discussions.
● List with the children singular nouns and discuss spelling of plurals.

Relevant published materials/resources

NLS Activity Resource Sheet

Year	3
Term	2
Strand	S 8

Objectives

Other uses of capitalisation from reading, e.g. names, headings, special emphasis, new lines, in poetry.

Activities

Group
- The children investigate and list all the instances of capital letters being used.
- From these lists draw up a class chart. Add to this when new instances are found, e.g.

> **We investigated capital letters and found that they are used in many places.**
>
> Whenever you write I.
> For people's names - John, Sanjay.
> For days of the week - Monday.
> For place names - Brighton.
> When you start a sentence.
> In poetry, when writers start a line.

There are four names without capital letters. Can you find them?

Plenary
- Ask the children to report back to the whole class.
- Challenge the children by setting a task:
Can you find at least ten different reasons for using a capital letter?
- When marking children's work, indicate where capitals have not been used correctly by saying or writing:
There are four capital letters missing - please find them
- Vary the amount of help given depending on the child.

Relevant published materials/resources

© Crown copyright 1998

NLS Activity Resource Sheet

Objectives

To experiment with deleting words in sentences to see which are essential to retain meaning and which are not.

Activities

Shared or Group activity

● Pretend you are the editor of a newspaper. Provide a lengthy passage and instruct the children that there is only room for 100 words. They must get out the editor's red pen and delete all unnecessary words, phrases or sentences. Show them how, if in doubt, they should delete the words and then re-read to check whether the essential meaning has been retained.

● List sentences and show how they can be trimmed, for instance in order to send a vital *message in a bottle*; e.g.

> Do you think that you would be most awfully kind and send me one of those very sharp kitchen knives as soon as you are able.

could become:

> Send knives!

● Play 'SHRINK ME', in which sentences have swallowed a potion to shrink them. Children have to shorten each sentence. The winner is the child who retains the meaning but has the smallest word count.

● Use colour coded words to create long sentences that have to be shrunk. Consider what sorts of words can be removed and what types are essential.

Relevant published materials/resources

NLS Activity Resource Sheet

Year	3
Term	2
Strand	S 9

Objectives

To experiment with deleting words in sentences to see which are essential to retain meaning and which are not.

Activities

Class and Group

- In Shared Reading, use 'Post-Its' to mask out words or phrases that add colour, leaving essential words, or to mask out the essential words.
- On a passage children delete words that add colour, leaving the essential words.
- In non-fiction reading the children circle or highlight key words, phrases or sentences that are essential to understanding the text.
- Use a poem that is descriptive and ask the children to take out descriptive language leaving just the bare meaning. Compare with non-fiction. Does poetry tend to use more words and phrases that add colour but are not essential to meaning?
- Send the class a 'secret message' that is very over-written. The task is to extract the essence of the message, as they can only send a target number of words on with their secret messenger.
- Use colour-coded words to create sentences. Which colours can be removed and yet the sense is retained?

Relevant published materials/resources

© Crown copyright 1998

NLS Activity Resource Sheet

Year	3
Term	2
Strand	T 17

Objectives

To explore ways of writing ideas, messages, etc. in shortened forms, e.g. notes, lists, headlines, telegrams; to understand that some words are more essential to meaning than others.

Activities

Class or Group

● Demonstrate how to take notes by using a shared text and circling the key points.

● Practise writing brief messages that contain only the essential words that are needed through activities such as:

- Creating newspaper headlines for well-known traditional stories.
- Sending 'telegrams' from a character in a story who is in trouble, e.g. 'Trapped in witch's house, middle of woods. Gretel'. Limit children to a maximum of ten words.
- Sending a 'message in a bottle' from a fictional character or a message attached to a pigeon's leg.
- Give children an elaborate message and they have to trim it down to an essential ten words. (They only have £1 and it costs 10p a word!)
- List key points in non-fiction.
- Write a news account but limit children to 50 words. You are a mean editor!

Relevant published materials/resources

NLS Activity Resource Sheet

Year	3
Term	3
Strand	S 2

Objectives

To identify pronouns and understand their functions in sentences.

Activities

Class

● In Shared Reading, explain and point out pronouns, in a passage, as a substitute for nouns.

Group

● Collect and list pronouns. Try substituting pronouns for nouns in sentences.
● In a short passage take out all the nouns and insert pronouns, can it be understood?
● Alternatively, in a short passage use no pronouns. This soon shows why we use pronouns as it sounds very tedious and repetitive.
● Write poetic sentences based on a repeating phrases, *he is*, *she is* or *you are*, e.g.

> She is a silver star slinking into the night.
> She is like a flower of light.
> She is like a silent pair of lips, saying something unknown.
> She is found in a blade of grass.
> She is frosted in ice.

Relevant published materials/resources

NLS Activity Resource Sheet

Year	3
Term	3
Strand	S 2

Objectives

To identify pronouns and understand their functions in sentences.

N.B.
See **Y3 T3 T3**

Activities

Class

● In Shared Reading, using different examples, point out the use of first person and third person in narrative. Discuss differences with children. Who is writing the story? What is the effect on the reader of first or third person? Which do they prefer reading and writing?
● In Shared Writing demonstrate how first person can be turned to third person by transforming a prepared passage. Compare both passages and discuss the impact. Which works best and why?

Group

● In Guided Reading, select and list well-known stories on basis of first or third person viewpoint. List viewpoint, character's name and a typical sentence. Which is more popular? Prepare for the class plenary.
● In Group Writing, transform a prepared passage or a selected passage from children's own reading book from first to third person or vice versa.
● Write a story or short extract in the first person, perhaps in diary form. Before writing stories, children should be asked to consider viewpoint.
● Transform an extract to first or third person from own reading book. Prepare a reading for the class plenary.

Plenary

Present and perform the work from the Guided Reading and Writing sessions.

Relevant published materials/resources

NLS Activity Resource Sheet

Year	3
Term	3
Strand	S 3

Objectives

To ensure grammatical agreement in speech and writing of pronouns and verbs, e.g. *I am*, *we are*, in Standard English.

Activities

Class

● Read aloud examples of a toddler's speech without subject/verb agreement, e.g. the Laura poems in Michael Rosen's **The Hypnotiser**.

● Ask the children to identify how the speech will change as the toddler grows older.

● Edit the speech in a Shared Writing activity. Use the terms 'verb', 'noun', 'pronoun' where appropriate.

● Consider the types of speech used to address different groups, e.g. **'The School Trip'** in **The Hypnotiser**. Use the text to examine the subject/verb agreements and discuss how it would be altered for a different target audience.

● Explain and chart common errors. Ask children to proof-read for these.

> Wah! Me want din-dins!

> I would like my dinner now please, as I'm rather hungry!

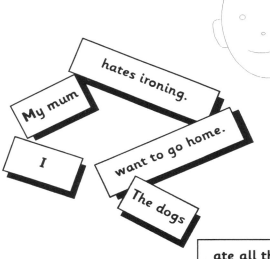

My mum hates ironing.

I want to go home.

The dogs ate all the bones.

Group

● Use the Photocopiable Resource Sheets to play *Snap* and *Pelmanism* to match subject and sentence cards.

● Use the cards to make silly sentences flip books, and illustrate them.

● Give the children written examples of toddler speech to edit.

Relevant published materials/resources

The Grammar and Punctuation Book, Pie Corbett (Stanley Thornes): refer to Copymasters 31/32; **The Hypnotiser**, Michael Rosen (Young Lions); **Grammar Rules** (Collins Ed.).

NLS Activity Resource Sheet

Year	3
Term	3
Strand	S 3

Objectives

To ensure grammatical agreement in speech and writing of pronouns and verbs, e.g. *I am*, *we are*, in standard English.

Activities

Class or Group
- Identify and list singular/plural persons and verb agreements.
- Proof-read a short, prepared passage and circle where the person/verb agreements are incorrect, e.g. *we was running*.
- Collect instances from everyday speech and list these beside the standard written form.
- Encourage the children to proof-read for errors of disagreement. When commenting on written work, get the children to find and change any such errors in their work.

Relevant published materials/resources

NLS Activity Resource Sheet

Year	3
Term	3
Strand	S 5

Objectives

How sentences can be joined in more complex ways through using a widening range of conjunctions in addition to 'and', and 'then', e.g. *if, so, while, though, since, when*.

Activities

Shared or Group activity

- Identify and list as many conjunctions as possible. Note conjunctions in Shared Reading and add to the list. Demonstrate how conjunctions 'join' sentences, like a railway junction.
- Give children lists of simple sentences. These can be cut up, glued onto a sheet and joined with a selected conjunction, e.g.

Tom is clean.

It runs smoothly.

The car starts.

He is kind.

- For each new sentence only certain conjunctions will work. Discuss different shades of meaning, e.g. *I woke early but ... and ... then I missed the postman*.
- List a simple sentence. Children extend the sentence in five different ways using different conjunctions, e.g.

> I woke early - although I was still tired.
> I woke early - because the ship's crew made such a noise.
> I woke early - during the winter because it was so cold ... etc.

- Investigate not using 'and' or 'then'. These tend to invite or support simple forms of thinking. As soon as a word like 'however' or 'because' is used a more complex form of thinking is demanded. Therefore more interesting and complex sentences are created.
- Use cloze procedure with conjunctions omitted.
- Give the children a passage where either 'and' or 'then' is overused. In pairs, they should edit to remove as many as is sensible, to improve the narrative.
- When marking proactively, suggest that children return to an overuse of 'and' to remove it where it is sensible.
- When reading, identify examples of different conjunctions. Explain the demands a conjunction makes, e.g. *'Because' means you have to explain; 'Then' means you can say what happened next*, etc.

Relevant published materials/resources

© Crown copyright 1998

NLS Activity Resource Sheet

Year	3
Term	3
Strand	S 5

Objectives

How sentences can be joined in more complex ways through using a widening range of conjunctions in addition to 'and' and 'then', e.g. *if, so, while, though, since, when.*

Activities

Class
- Introduce *Boring sentences.*
- Provide a list of simple and dull sentences and experiment with different ways of enlivening them.
- Who can make the most interesting sentences using a range of conjunctions.

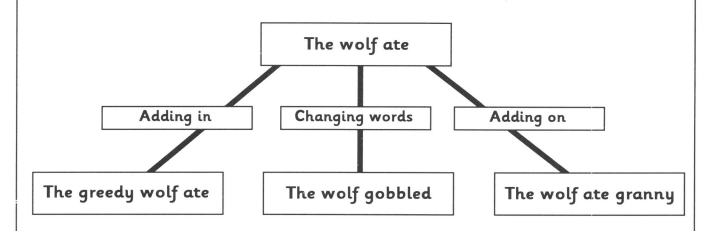

Group
- The children attempt their own *Boring sentences.*
- Move on to using several sentences or a short passage.
- Avoid rewriting by children revising passages.
- Demonstarte how to use a range of conjunctions to extend sentences, e.g. 'The wolf ate granny because ...'..

Relevant published materials/resources

NLS Activity Resource Sheet

Year	3
Term	3
Strand	S 6

Objectives

To investigate through reading and writing how words and phrases can signal time sequences.

Activities

Shared or Group Reading
- Children investigate a range of texts and list words that signal time sequences, e.g. *first*, *then*, *next*, *after*, *meanwhile*, *from*, *where*.
- Create inventive and imaginative sentences, e.g.

> During Winter the snow clutches the streets.
> Before the Autumn the sun drinks the earth's cocktail.
> After midnight the moon shivers till dawn.
> Later than tomorrow is soon enough for eternity . . .

- Link to work looking at the structure of recounts.
- Demonstrate use in Shared Writing.
- Link to work in non-fiction in **T16** and **T22**.

Relevant published materials/resources

NLS Activity Resource Sheet

Year	4
Term	1
Strand	S 1

Objectives

To re-read own writing to check for grammatical sense (coherence) and accuracy (agreement); to identify errors and suggest alternative constructions.

Activities

1. Teacher writes part of a story/a piece of information, writing at children's dictation, including any non-standard English.

3. If teacher guidance needs to be more specific, try the following type of questions:
Let's try and think of other ways to say 'and then'. Here are some of our ideas. Which shall we choose?
Let's read the story again and see if we can find out who she is in this part.
This part seems to end rather quickly and it isn't clear what the brave knight did.

2. Teacher encourages and acts on children's suggestions, continually inviting re-reading and reflection, e.g.
Is everyone happy with this sentence?
Is there a way of making it even better?
Does everything in this sentence make sense?
Are there any words we could make more interesting?

4. Use opportunities to replace non-standard forms after discussion and collect non-standard written forms to be used as a checklist, e.g. *They was; could of; us be, you'm,* depending on area of country.

- Prepare a piece of writing that lacks cohesion and agreement and work on it with children.
- Demonstrate simple ways of improving texts and ask children to use strategies when revising their own or others' work, e.g.

> You can add in words – *The dog ... the shaggy dog.*
> You can change words – *The dog went (ran) down the road.*
> You can name common nouns – *The dog (dachshund) ran down the road.*
> You can extend sentences – *The shaggy dog ran down the road because ...*
> You can trim and reorganise sentences or whole sections.

Group
- Work as a group on prepared texts that contain errors.
- In Guided Writing, help children to focus on an aspect by indicating on the board what you are going to be looking for in their writing, e.g. alternatives to *and* or *then*. Discuss alternatives, including punctuation or writing shorter sentences.
- Develop the use of response partners. Use a response checklist (relevant to text type) with their own text.
- Ask children to design checklists for other genres, using examples of written genres to discuss differences in organisation, cohesion and grammar.

Relevant published materials/resources

Writing Frames, Maureen Lewis and David Wray (Reading, Language and Information Centre, University of Reading). **Write Ways**, Lesley WingJan (OUP).
See **Photocopiable Resource Sheets** for responding to different types of writing.

© Crown copyright 1998

NLS Activity Resource Sheet

Year	4
Term	1
Strand	S 2

Objectives

To understand the term 'tense' (i.e. that it refers to time) in relation to verbs and use it appropriately; understand that one test of whether a word is a verb is whether or not its tense can be changed.

Activities

Shared or Group activity
- Use the term tense during Shared Reading, checking which tense passages are written in. Encourage children to use the term.
- Reinforce the notion of tense through such activities as changing lists of verbs from one tense to another.
- Write weekend news on Monday. On Tuesday change this into the present tense, as if part of a story.
- List future hopes' *In the future I shall ...*'. Use this to set targets, e.g. *'to improve my writing I shall try to ...'*.
- In a prepared passage circle verbs in the past tense in red, present in green and future in blue.
- List and categorise words that change when used in the past tense and words that do not change, e.g.

> fly - flew
> run - ran
> catch - caught
> takes - took
> am - was
> slip - slipped
> trip - tripped
> chat - chatted
> hop - hopped
> love - loved
> talk - talked
> cook - cooked
> smile - smiled

- Begin to consider/notice ways in which spellings change in relation to categories, e.g. doubling of the final consonant in *tip - tipped*.
- Apply the 'can the tense be changed?' test to decide if words in a list/sentence are verbs.

Relevant published materials/resources

© Crown copyright 1998

NLS Activity Resource Sheet

Year	4
Term	1
Strand	S 2

Objectives

To revise work on verbs from Year1 term 3 and to investigate verb tenses.

Activities

Shared or Group Writing

- Write a memory poem to focus on past tense, e.g.

> When I was young . . .
> A while ago I . . .
> I used to . . .
> I remember when . . .

- Write list poems for the present (I like . . ., I hate . . .) and the future (when I am older I will . . .)
- List verbs under headings of past, present, future.
- Identify in reading books, examples of past, present, future. Collect and list. Discuss effects on word order.
- Change a passage from present to past and vice versa.
- Collect verbs into three boxes denoting what you used to do, do now and would like to do, e.g.

> Past: cried, gurgled, bubbled, toddled
> Present: writes, reads, runs, plays
> Future: will work, will travel, will go shopping.

- Use cloze procedure to reinforce the notion of consistency in tenses.

Relevant published materials/resources

NLS Activity Resource Sheet

Year	4
Term	1
Strand	S 2

Objectives

To compare sentences from narrative and information texts, e.g. narrative in past tense, explanations in present tense (e.g. *when the circuit is ...*'); forecasts, directions, etc. in future. Develop awareness of how tense relates to purpose and structure of text.

Activities

Shared or Group Reading

● Let children investigate different types of texts giving examples of sentences and discover typically the verb tense used, e.g. compare school story, historical story, adventure story, science fiction.

● Compare narrative with forms of non-fiction, e.g. reports, recounts, exposition, explanation, instruction. Chart findings, e.g. *in recounts you use past tense because . . .*

● Look at examples from letters, magazines, newspapers, diaries, etc. and label past, present or future.

● Children create wall charts to begin to define or explain when and how verb tenses are used, listing examples, e.g.

> 'You need the past tense when ...'
> 'A list of texts that use past tense ...'
> 'When you use the past tense the verb ...'

● Use cloze procedure to consider appropriate tenses for different types of text.

● Revise texts where tenses are muddled or inappropriately used.

Relevant published materials/resources

NLS Activity Resource Sheet

Year	4
Term	1
Strand	S 2

Objectives

To revise work on verbs from Year 3 term 1 and to investigate verb tenses (past, present, future).

Activities

Shared or Group activity

● In pairs play a game where one child speaks in the present tense and their partner has to turn the statement into the past or future, e.g.

> "I eat a big banana."
> "I ate a big banana."
> "I will eat a big banana."

● Transform a section from a reading book or a prepared passage into a different tense. Pairs of children could check each other's writing for consistent use of the same tense.
● Use cloze procedure to practise consistency in tenses.
● Write short extracts of narrative in past or present tense, based on models from reading.
● Compare text types and consider the technical use of tense, e.g. recounts in the past tense.
● Discuss how tense relates to the purpose of the text.
● Use the word 'tense' in context to encourage children to use it.
● Discuss how one test of a 'verb' is whether or not its tense can be changed.

Relevant published materials/resources

NLS Activity Resource Sheet

Objectives

To revise work on verbs from Year 1 term 3.

Activities

Shared or Group activity
- Read through a passage circling the verbs.
- Let children alter the verbs. This can lead to amusing results if the 'wrong' verb is used. Who can find verbs which almost mean the same as the original?
- Replace verbs with invented verbs, for instance, based on the names of animals, e.g.

> We lioned out loud.
> The teacher snaked and owled at us.
> We kangarooed away . . .

- Create a verb alphabet, e.g. *ask, buy*, etc.
- Read, identify and collect verbs under different headings such as, favourite verbs, frightening verbs, verbs that sound funny, etc.
- Mask out verbs in a shared text and discuss as a class what each might be.
- List synonymous verbs for common verbs such as *take, see, steal, make, run, eat*.
- When writing and revising challenge children to select verbs carefully so that they use powerful and expressive verbs to enliven sentences.
- By circling verbs in one colour, investigate and discover where they usually lie in a sentence – compare narrative and instructions, etc.
- Use cloze procedure, omitting verbs.
- Continue to identify in reading the effective use of verbs. List and investigate their use in writing.
- Pro-actively mark by underlining the weak use of verbs, so that children are given the opportunity to revise and improve.
- Work on sentences or passages of writing where verbs have been purposefully written lacking in power. Ask children to circle, highlight or underline weak or inappropriate use of verbs before altering.

Relevant published materials/resources

NLS Activity Resource Sheet

Year	4
Term	1
Strand	S 3

Objectives

To identify the use of powerful verbs.

Activities

Shared or Group Reading/Writing

● List together, in pairs or individually, as quickly as possible, as many alternative verbs as you can think of to fit into different sentences, e.g.

> Sally turned round and said/spoke/cried/yelled ...
> The donkey escaped and ran/staggered/hopped ...
> John saw the orange and took/grabbed/snatched
> She turned and looked/stared/gazed ...
> The candle flame leaned/blew/danced/shimmered ...
> The wind blew/blasted/whipped/whistled ... etc.

● When children are writing encourage them to select verbs carefully. Use a dotted line when marking pro-actively to ask children to reconsider their choice of verb, making it more powerful and expressive or precise.
● List families of synonymous verbs. Search in the thesaurus to discover which verbs have many alternatives.
Design verb 'plants' which contain flowers showing alternatives, e.g.

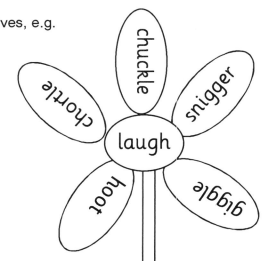

Relevant published materials/resources

NLS Activity Resource Sheet

Year	4
Term	1
Strand	S 5

Objectives

To practise using commas to mark grammatical boundaries within sentences; link to work on editing and revising own writing.

Activities

Shared and Group activity

● Identify over time, and let the children discover and note instances, of how commas are used. Let the children begin to generate their own explanations. Refine these through investigating, in reading, how commas are used, and experimenting in writing.

● Consider commas in a list. Find and share instances. Fill in missing commas from a prepared passage. Write 'five things you might find in a wizard's cave, a mermaid's purse ... ', e.g.

> In a mermaid's purse you might find a drowned sailor's ring, a starfish, a song sheet, a golden comb and a mirror of truth.

● Investigate commas used in dialogue, e.g. *"I will not wait for long,"* *muttered Janet.*

● Consider commas used for a 'pause', e.g. *John, who was not very kind, stared at the dog.*

● Notice instances of using commas and add to a wall chart, categorise and cite instances.

● When marking work, indicate if commas are omitted, suggesting how many and in which sentences.

● Practise proof reading on prepared passages concentrating on commas.

● When proof reading, ask the children to read work aloud, listening for a pause, as well as using wall charts that define or explain when commas should be used.

● Practise proof reading on prepared passages that have all the commas omitted.

● Have fun working as a group on a punctuated poem. To do this, children need copies of a poem on which they identify punctuation marks, including commas. Each mark is given a sound, e.g. a hand clap for an exclamation mark or a hiss for a comma. Ask a group to practise and perform this. Which group chose the most appropriate sounds for different marks? Did the sounds add to the meaning and rhythm of the poem?

Relevant published materials/resources

NLS Activity Resource Sheet

Objectives

To revise and extend work on adjectives from Y3 term 2.

Activities

Shared or Group activity
- Create 'adjective' plants, where the stem is a noun and each leaf is a possible adjective.
- Underline, circle or highlight the adjectives in a passage.
- Prepare a passage with too many adjectives for children to read critically and delete some or all, deciding what is needed, e.g.

> The small, slight, thin, slender, graceful, tiny cat ...

- Prepare a cloze procedure with adjectives omitted or leave space so children have to insert an adjective.
- List adjectives to describe an alphabet of animals, e.g. *awful ant, bold baboon, curious crocodile.*
- List synonymous adjectives for nouns, e.g. *fat/lumpy/large/thick/plump fingers, etc.*
- When writing or revising, discuss possible use of adjectives. Push children to select carefully and not necessarily write the first one that comes into their minds!
- To develop work on settings, take clipboards and go outside. Focus on possible settings. List what can be seen (nouns) and then begin listing possible adjectives, e.g.

> tree - tall, thin, ancient ...
> car - sleek, shiny, blue ...
> bike - wobbly, rusty ...

- Use adjectives (and verbs) to help write simple lists and descriptions.
- Identify in reading, and collect effective descriptions of, settings, characters, events and the weather.

Relevant published materials/resources

NLS Activity Resource Sheet

Objectives

To revise and extend work on adjectives from Y3 term 2 and link to work on expressive and figurative language in stories and poetry.

Activities

Shared and Group activity

- Consciously use the terms 'noun' and 'adjective' and encourage children to do so.
- Continue quick activities to focus on categorising words in sentences, e.g. underlining adjectives used in a menu or holiday brochure. Writing their own versions.
- Draw children's attention to proper nouns in reading. What would it have sounded like if the writer had used a common noun? Decide which communicates more clearly, e.g.

'The man climbed into the car', or
'The Prime Minister climbed into the Rolls Royce'.

- List sentences with common nouns and introduce the idea of 'naming' words, e.g. see opposite.
- When writing in front of children be aware of selecting proper nouns so that you 'name' nouns and thereby help the reader to 'picture' what you are writing about, e.g. see opposite.
- When marking children's writing indicate where a common noun could be replaced by proper noun.
- When children's writing is read aloud encourage those listening to spot the weak use of adjectives and common nouns. They should be able to turn *The fish leaped* into *The shark leaped* or *The minnow leaped*.
- Children to investigate and list nouns which need a capital letter. Create simple wall charts to pool findings.
- Continue to collect and pair adjectives and nouns. Discuss the use of description and its impact in reading. Revise passages to ensure effective use of adjectives.

> The bird sat on the tree
> could become
>   the robin sat on the fir tree
> or
>   the vulture sat on the holly bush.

> The man went to the town
> could become,
>   Dick Whittington went to London
> or
>   Nigel went to Neasden.

Relevant published materials/resources

NLS Activity Resource Sheet

Year	4
Term	2
Strand	S 1

Objectives

To revise and extend work on adjectives from Y3 term 2 and link to work on expressive and figurative language in stories and poetry.

Activities

Shared or Group activity

- When discussing reading and writing use, and encourage the children to use, the term 'adjective'. Identify and list effective examples from reading.
- Read sentences aloud and ask the children to identify effective use of words:

> "What was the good adjective in the sentence?"
> "Which word was well chosen?"

- When reading, encourage the children to savour and even re-read to give emphasis, any good examples of adjectives and other words.
- When marking, indicate well chosen adjectives. Use a dotted line to indicate where a word has been repeated or a more effective choice is needed, e.g.

> The big shark opened its big mouth and I saw its big teeth.

- Take a limited focus, something that everyone can see, or which is very familiar, e.g. *a candle flame, the moon, a plant, etc*. List with the class, as many adjectives as possible. Push children to give choices, e.g. *red, scarlet, crimson flame.*
- In pairs, give the children a number of objects and ask them to brainstorm and list possible adjectives. Circle favourites and use these to write simple descriptions.
- Use cloze procedures with adjectives omitted. Discuss the best choice and whether one is needed.
- Discuss over use of adjectives and instances where adjectives are not needed, e.g. *The hot sun blazed.*
- Discuss using adjectives to add new information, to surprise the reader or particularise a noun.

Relevant published materials/resources

NLS Activity Resource Sheet

Objectives

Examining comparative and superlative adjectives.

Activities

Shared or Group Writing
- List comparatives in three simple columns.

Large   larger   largest.
Small   smaller   smallest.

- Change sentences, working in threes and passing them round, e.g. *Tom is funny. Jane is funnier. Sally is funniest.*
- Investigate persuasive writing, including adverts and TV adverts. List sentences where comparatives are used to persuade, e.g. *the best, the cheapest, the fastest, cleaner than ..., smoother than ...*
- Write a comparative poem – see opposite.
- Write a boastful poem about a mythical or invented creature – see opposite.
- Use comparatives and comparative language –*very, much, more, most*, etc. – to advertise yourself or a friend , e.g.

He is funnier than Lenny Henry on a banana skin.
He is slimmer than a stick insect on a diet.
He is angrier than a bull who sees a red packet of beefburgers in a shopping bag.

> **For sale**
> The friendliest girl in the class.
> Joanna is kinder than you will believe.
> She is better at washing up than any machine and her room will be the tidiest!
> All this and more, much more when you purchase the cheapest and yet most wonderful Joanna.
> **50p or nearest offer!**

The Zegreb is:
faster than a jet-powered cheetah,
larger than the Sun's father,
cleverer than Einstein's teacher,
quieter than a needle dropped on velvet,
more cunning than a fox who has joined MENSA.

Relevant published materials/resources

© Crown copyright 1998

NLS Activity Resource Sheet

Objectives

To use the apostrophe accurately to mark possession.

> **N.B.**
> Apostrophe for omission
> is found in **Y3 T2, 3;
> W 11,15**

Activities

Shared and Group Reading

- Notice, highlight or circle instances where apostrophes occur.
- Collect and list instances where apostrophe is used instead of a letter/s, e.g.

> don't - do not
> shan't - shall not
> can't - cannot

- Explain apostrophes used for possession. Children should look for and list instances in the following way:

> John's car - the car of John.
> The rook's nest - the nest of the rook.
> The lions' meat - the meat of the lions.

- Use the question 'To whom does it belong?' as a 'test' to help children understand the function of the apostrophe.

Relevant published materials/resources

NLS Activity Resource Sheet

Objectives

Distinguishing between uses of apostrophes for contraction and possession; beginning to use the apostrophe appropriately in their own writing.

Activities

Shared or Group activity

● Children in groups investigate apostrophes in a given passage or reading books. Prepare a poster to explain/define, or a presentation for the plenary session. They should explain different uses of apostrophes in:

> omission, e.g. don't - do not
>
> possession, e.g. Jane's ring.

● They should explain where the apostrophe lies depending on singular (Jane's) or plural (girls') noun.
● Children work through a prepared passage, proof reading for apostrophes. Remind them to use the 'belonging' test, e.g. *it was Jane's car - the car of Jane.*
● Add apostrophes to a proof reading checklist for those children who are confident in its use.
● Draw attention to one notable exception:

> it's - it is
> its collar - the collar of it
> (no apostrophe).

● Collect and list other examples of apostrophe use that show omission, e.g. *o'clock, on the 'phone, etc.*
● When marking constructively, consider the list opposite.

(1) Explain to those who over-use apostrophes that they should look at specific instances of apostrophe use in reading/writing. Work in a group. Secure an understanding of omission before moving on to possession. (Revise singular/plural).
(2) Ask those who understood but have been careless, to check for missing apostrophes.
(3) Ask those who are still trying to apply their understanding, to 'check for three instances where an apostrophe is missing'.
(4) To help those less sure, number the apostrophes missing and put a star by the sentence where each is needed.

Relevant published materials/resources

© Crown copyright 1998

NLS Activity Resource Sheet

Year	4
Term	2
Strand	S 3

Objectives

To understand the significance of word order, e.g. some re-orderings destroy meaning; some make sense but change meaning; sentences can be re-ordered to retain meaning (sometimes adding words); subsequent words are governed by preceding ones.

Activities

Class or Group

- Cut up a poem verse by verse, couplet by couplet, line by line or a haiku, word by word. Discuss possible new combinations.
- Children cut up a short passage and put it back together to create something new, possibly quite silly.
- Put words and phrases onto blank playing cards. Let the children play with words to create sentences that might fit:

> - a story;
> - a poem;
> - an advert;
> - an instruction;
> - a report;
> - a recount, etc.

- List ten sentences. Cut them in half. The children reassemble them in different ways. They can change words, or add new words. Who can make the funniest piece of writing? Who can make the most sensible new piece of writing?
- Use a collection of words on strips of card to create very long sentences. Ask the children if their partners can make the sentences shorter. Which words can be taken out leaving the basic meaning unaltered?

Relevant published materials/resources

NLS Activity Resource Sheet

Year	4
Term	2
Strand	S 3

Objectives

To understand the significance of word order, e.g. some re-orderings destroy meanings; some make sense but change meaning (sometimes adding words); subsequent words are governed by preceding ones.

Activities

Class or Group

● Take a piece of writing. Cut up sentences and jumble the order. Ask the children to re-order the sentences into a logical or chronological flow so that they make sense. Contrast poetry with a different genre, such as instructional writing. Consider how order is vital to meanings.

● When writing in front of the class demonstrate how words can be changed, word order altered or sentences moved to create different effects. Show the children how to use arrows and brackets to indicate revision changes.

● Give the children drafts to revise and improve. Discuss in the plenary session any suggested changes.

● Cut-up sequence of sentences to re-order using instructions where the correct order matters or poetry where it may matter less.

Relevant published materials/resources

NLS Activity Resource Sheet

Objectives

To identify how and why paragraphs are used to organise and sequence information.

Activities

Shared or Group activity

- Notice in reading how paragraphs are used. In non-fiction identify the function of each paragraph: 'What it tells us', 'What it is about'.
- When writing create headings for each paragraph in non-fiction. List points or facts to include under each heading. Write paragraphs using notes. Demonstrate before letting children try this.
- Let children organise a jumbled set of information notes under headings.
- Children check paragraphs to see if the correct information is in the correct paragraph.
- Re-read paragraphs to check points are in order and there is a logical progression in the sentences.
- Create charts listing reasons for using paragraphs in narrative.
- Reorganise a set of jumbled paragraphs.
- Link to non-fiction work by creating frameworks from reading different texts, deciding headings for each paragraph. Model using frameworks in writing to show how to plan under headings and how to write paragraphs from notes.

Relevant published materials/resources

NLS Activity Resource Sheet

Year	4
Term	3
Strand	S 1

Objectives

To understand that some words can be changed in particular ways and others cannot e.g. changing verb endings, adding comparative endings, pluralisation, etc., and that these are important clues for identifying parts of word classes.

Activities

Shared or Group Reading

● Collect the most common endings that can be added on to words and list examples, e.g. *s, es, ed, ing, ly, er, est*.

● What do the children notice about the different columns? What sort of words come into the *s, es* groups? What type of words is listed under *ed, ing*? What about *er* and *est*?

● Link to work on spelling. Create charts.

● Use colour-coded words to support children who need to revisit word classes before categorising words by changes in spelling.

Relevant published materials/resources

NLS Activity Resource Sheet

Year	4
Term	3
Strand	S 3

Objectives

To understand how the grammar of a sentence alters when the sentence type is altered, e.g. a statement is made to a question, a question becomes an order, a positive statement is made negative.

Activities

Shared and Group activity

- Identify negatives in sentences. Which words or parts of words need to be taken out to make the sentence positive? Collect and list negative words, e.g. *no, neither, nothing, nobody, never, not* and prefixes, e.g. *un-, mis-, non-*. List words using negative prefixes.
- Give children sentences, and then a passage, to transform, positive to negative or vice versa. This can be amusing, for instance, by transforming advertising slogans, e.g.

The powder that is not guaranteed to keep you clean. Feel dreadful about yourself in the slowest car ever invented, etc.

- List positive and negative views or points about different aspects, e.g.

> 'Five positive things about school'.
> 'Five negative points about the new motorway'.
> 'Five negative points about smoking', etc.

- Read **Nothingmas Day** by Adrian Mitchell. Attempt own version in writing about a different subject.
- Practise altering sentence types in Shared Writing, considering what
  - happens when sentences are altered, noting:
  - the order of words;
  - verb tenses;
  - additions and/or deletion of words;
  - changes to punctuation.

Relevant published materials/resources

Nothingmas Day, Adrian Mitchell – in **Balloon Lagoon** (Orchard Books).

NLS Activity Resource Sheet

Year	4
Term	3
Strand	S 3

Objectives

To understand how the grammar of a sentence alters when the sentence type is altered.

Activities

Shared or Group activity

- Investigate sentences, e.g. by searching for the shortest/the longest.
- Then list different types and create a wall chart, labelling the main types:

> statements,
> questions,
> exclamations (often introduced by 'what' or 'how'), and
> orders ('Put that down').

- Consider the difference between 'possibilities' and 'certainties', e.g.

> I might go to work - I am going to work.

- Provide short burst activities where children transform several sentences or a short passage, using suggested categories, e.g. from 'question' into 'statement'.
- Write questions before using non-fiction texts to seek answers.
- List statements of belief about poems or books being studied.
- List questions to ask a dragon, a mermaid, an alien, etc.
- List possibilities about poems or novels being studied.
- Transform dialogue questions to orders, working in pairs.
- Transform simple sentences by using different connectives.
- In pairs, generate questions and imaginative or factual answers, e.g.

> How hot is the sun?
> The sun is as hot as an explosion of curry in a furnace.

- In pairs, write affirmatives and negatives, e.g.

> What I like about mint is its freshness.
> What I do not like about mint is that it tastes like toothpaste.

Relevant published materials/resources

NLS Activity Resource Sheet

Objectives

To understand the basic conventions of standard English and consider when and why standard English is used.

Activities

N.B.
It is important to teach standard English and acknowledge the organisation of language in non-standard dialects.

Group

- Collect different ways of saying the same things.

> Shopkeeper: "Good morning, can I help you?"
> Policeman: "'ello, 'ello, 'ello."
> Friend: "Hiya."
> Teacher: "Good morning children."

- Read a range of short texts representing language varieties.
- Discuss differences between non-standard forms and standard English.
- Collect non-standard forms for a checklist. Some will be local, therefore lists may vary in different areas. See the Photocopiable Resource Sheet.
- Use a series of questions about standard English and writing when drafting and editing to self-monitor work. See the Photocopiable Resource Sheet.
- Discuss the need for standard English in formal, written contexts. If necessary list such situations, e.g. 'We use standard English when ...'.
- Explore the difference between informal spoken English and standard written English.

Relevant published materials/resources

NLS Activity Resource Sheet

Objectives

To discuss, edit and proof-read their own writing for clarity and correctness, e.g. by creating more complex sentences, using a range of connectives, simplifying clumsy constructions.

N.B.
Clumsy constructions are usually evidence of experimentation and therefore can provide opportunities for development.

Activities

Class

- Discuss models of text, particularly using information texts, examining passages for clarity and discussing whether they could be improved.
- Review some information books for the current class topic in relation to:

> - clarity of features supporting the finding of information
> - clarity of text to read.

- Look up the same information in a range of texts and compare the texts for effectiveness.
- Encourage whole class discussion on a range of writing examples. What could be alternative ways of writing them?
- When returning work, read examples aloud and encourage the children to identify strengths and areas to improve.
- When marking, pro-actively prompt the children to improve their writing with specific suggestions and indicate specific areas of success.

Group

- Children should discuss each other's writing, particularly parts which are unclear, in both fiction and information writing.
- Discuss the relative merits and appropriateness of brief sentences and longer ones. Take an opportunity to look at how longer complex sentences need to be clearer.
- Read completed drafts round the group for comments. The children identify what is successful as well as places that need improvement.
- Revise and proof-read in pairs.

Relevant published materials/resources

Non-fiction Big Books available from publishers include **Magic Bean** (Heinemann), **Literacy Links** (Kingscourt), **Book Project** (Longman).

NLS Activity Resource Sheet

Year	5
Term	1
Strand	S 5

Objectives

To understand the difference between direct and reported speech.

Activities

Class

- Ask children to 'act out' the speech parts of dialogue. A 'reporter' or 'shadow' stands behind and paraphrases the speech afterwards, e.g. *The wolf said he would huff and puff and blow the house down.* Use a simple playscript text.
- The teacher needs to transcribe so the text can be compared and contrasted, e.g.

Direct	Reported
The wolf said, "I'll huff and puff and blow the house down."	The wolf said he would huff and puff and blow the house down.

Group

- Hunt for directed and reported speech and classify. Extend this by transforming directed to reported and back again.
- Match sentence strips and classify.

- Colour the parts that stay constant. Discuss aspects that change, e.g. person, tense (sometimes), speech marks; added words.
- Relate altered tenses to altered persons and time scales.

> I changes to **he**
> **will** changes to **would**
> **present** tenses change to the **past**

- Groups could make their own strips to match given direct or reported speech.
- Transform short passages including direct speech to entirely indirect speech.
- In the course of writing brief sections of narrative ask children to write entirely without, or with, direct speech.

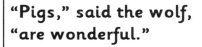

Plenary

- Share examples and evaluate.

Relevant published materials/resources

© Crown copyright 1998

NLS Activity Resource Sheet

Objectives

To understand the need for punctuation as an aid to the reader, e.g. commas to mark grammatical boundaries; a colon to signal, e.g. a list.

Activities

Group

● Use published and prepared texts of fiction, poetry and information to discuss features of punctuation.

● Select passages from a book and make a key using different symbols for punctuation. Children should work out what the symbols represent.

+mr£ +lee had lost his job and it was really hard to find a new one£
+at first he sat and cursed at the +t+v or threw slippers at the dog£
+it was the day +china%s mum said *#+i won%t be home till late* +john^ could you make the dinner$#
+she was just starting up in business* in partnership with her brother£ =+china%s uncle +tony* famous for his martial arts high kicks£ +he was the only one of +china%s uncles who regularly switched the light off with his big toe£=+they were going into the computer business£

From **China Lee** by Sue Limb.

Key:
+
£
%
*
#
^
$
=

● Practise proof-reading for punctuation as a whole class and in Guided Writing.
● Give groups a 'draft' that lacks punctuation. Differentiate this for different groups.
● Give groups a 'draft' where punctuation is muddled.
● Perform 'punctuated poems'.
● Try reading aloud passages with no punctuation or where punctuation is muddled.
● Ask children to investigate punctuation, write definitions and apply these.
● Model the use of punctuation and proof-reading.

Relevant published materials/resources

Punctuation activities based on suggestions from **Grammar and Punctuation 9–13,** Sue Hackman and Claire Humphreys (Hodder and Stoughton).

NLS Activity Resource Sheet

Year	5
Term	1
Strand	S 7

Objectives

From reading, to understand how dialogue is set out, e.g. on separate lines for alternate speakers in narrative, and the positioning of commas before speech marks.

Activities

Class
- Share extracts from different narrative and playscript sources, including some already read with the class, using a Big Book or multiple copies.
- Investigate dialogue in narrative. Discuss clues from the text as to who speaks, how they speak, etc.
- Investigate and chart:

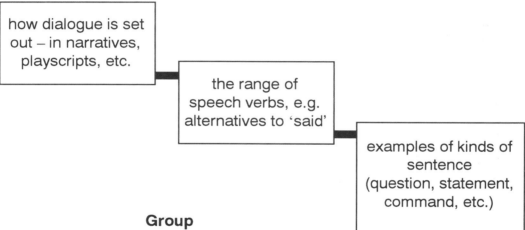

how dialogue is set out – in narratives, playscripts, etc.

the range of speech verbs, e.g. alternatives to 'said'

examples of kinds of sentence (question, statement, command, etc.)

Group
Children could:
- transcribe a section of dialogue into alternating speech bubbles;
- transcribe a narrative into a playscript or vice versa;
- carry out a speech verb word search. Collect verbs from skimming through different narrative texts; try to sort into different categories, e.g. by volume – *whisper, shout* – or by function – *question, statement;*
- compare how different authors favour setting out dialogue;
- use collections of speech verbs to match to collections of dialogue sentences. Which work and which do not? Why?
- demonstrate layout and punctuation, especially positioning of commas and the use of alternate lines.

Relevant published materials/resources

NLS Activity Resource Sheet

Year	5
Term	1
Strand	S 8

Objectives

To revise and extend work on verbs (see Y4 objectives) focusing on person ... experiment with transforming tense/form/person.

Activities

Shared or Group activity

● Take a few sentences in the first (I, we), second (you) and third (she/he/they) person. Show the children how to transform each with another person, considering any effect on other words, e.g.

> *I like ice cream.*

becomes

> *She likes ice cream.*

● Take short extracts from a biography or autobiography, e.g **Boy** by Roald Dahl, **Cider with Rosie** by Laurie Lee or **The Moon and I** by Betsy Byars, and transform into another person.
● Rewrite short events from stories using another character's viewpoint, e.g. 'I' becomes 'she'.
● Children could write their own autobiographical snippets of memorable experiences. Ask a partner to rewrite in the third person, transforming the extract into narrative/biography. Rewrite other children's memories as if they were a reporter, transforming 'I' into 'he' or 'she'.
● Children should check each other's work for agreement. Focus on this when constructively marking children's work.
● Prepare a cloze procedure, omitting pronouns. Children have to decide what person it might be from other words.
● Use cloze procedure, omitting verbs so that the children have to decide upon the correct agreement depending on pronoun.
● Investigate different text types to see where first, second, third person are typically used. Report back to the class, e.g. *In stories you usually find ... for instance ...*

Relevant published materials/resources

Boy, Roald Dahl (Puffin). **Cider with Rosie**, Laurie Lee (Penguin). **The Moon and I**, Betsy Byars (W Morrow).

© Crown copyright 1998

NLS Activity Resource Sheet

Objectives

To revise and extend work on verbs (see **Y4 T1** Sentence level objectives).

Activities

Class

● Using reading books, collect examples of tenses:
past, present and future.

Past	Present	Future
I was running I ran (I have run)	I am running I run	I will run I will be running

● Discuss the impact of 'trimming' verbs, e.g.
'The man was running.' 'The man ran.'

Group

● Experiment with transforming sentences into different tenses and see which words or parts of words change (the suffixes and the auxiliaries as in the box).
● Transform from first to third person.
● Sort sentences on strips into different groups by tense or person.
● Collect and list examples of effective use of verbs in writing.
● Select one verb and write a series of sentences appropriate to different genre, tenses or person, e.g.

am to **was**

have to **had**

Twist the wheel twice (Instruction).
Flames twist (Poetic).
The drill twists as the power is turned on (Report).

Relevant published materials/resources

NLS Activity Resource Sheet

Year	5
Term	1
Strand	S 9

Objectives

To identify the imperative form in instructional writing and the past tense in recounts and use this awareness when writing for these purposes.

Activities

Shared or Group activity

● Read examples of different text types and identify verb type and position. 'What can we say about the way verbs are being used in this report, recount, etc?'

● Double check initial observation in other examples. Children produce a chart that indicates text type/comment on verb/example, e.g.

Instructions	Sentences often start with verb.	Stir in sugar.
	Present or future tense.	You will need an egg.
	Sentences written as 'orders'.	Wait for two minutes.

● Devise cloze procedures of instructional/report writing, focusing on verb usage.

● Use information gathered about verbs to inform writing in different genres. Revise writing for appropriate verb usage.

● Use information gathered to 'play with genres'. For instance, writing a recipe for a good party, e.g.

> Take twenty children.
> Place in a warm room for two hours.
> Let the temperature rise.
> Stir in a conjuror and several rabbits in a hat.
> Let five overexcited children simmer.
> Top with a pinch of excitement.
> Serve with bulky presents and bright balloons.

Relevant published materials/resources

NLS Activity Resource Sheet

Year	5
Term	2
Strand	S 6

Objectives

To be aware of the differences between spoken and written language.

Activities

Shared or Group Reading

● Children list suggested differences between reading and telling. Are there any words, phrases or sentences that you would not use if you were telling the tale?

● Extract the 'bare bones' of the plot and use this to tell the tale in pairs, helping each other. Listen as a group or class to one retelling. List noticed differences, e.g.

> You can pause.
> You can repeat yourself.
> You use your eyes.
> You can use 'and' more often.
> You can use the tone of voice to show feelings and do not need to say, 'he said angrily'.
> You do not have to tell the reader so much.
> You can use gestures to act out parts that do not need writing down.

● Consider writing down stories and list conventions needed, e.g.

> Use punctuation to show ...
> Write in how people spoke to show ...
> Avoid unnecessary repetitions, etc.

Relevant published materials/resources

Tales, Myths and Legends, ed. Pie Corbett (Scholastic). **Traditional Storytelling in the Classroom**, Teresa Grainger (Scholastic).

NLS Activity Resource Sheet

Objectives

To explore ambiguities that arise from sentence contractions, e.g. through signs and headlines:
'*Police shot man with knife*', '*Nothing acts faster than Anadin*', '*Baby Changing Room*'.

Activities

Shared or Group Reading

● Scan adverts, news headlines and joke books to collect and list ambiguities.

● Take an example and generate more based on syntax of sentence e.g.

> Police shot man with knife.
>
> Girl kissed boy with sausage.
>
> Dog bit man with banana.

● Collect and list homonyms – words that have more than one meaning, e.g. watch. Use such words to create sentences where they are used in different ways, e.g.

> Watch out for my watch on the midnight watch.
> Let's wave at the waves.

Relevant published materials/resources

© Crown copyright 1998

NLS Activity Resource Sheet

Year	5
Term	2
Strand	S 8

Objectives

To construct sentences in different ways, while retaining meaning, through: combining two or more sentences; reordering them; deleting or substituting words; writing them in more telegraphic ways.

Activities

Shared and Group Writing

- Demonstrate and practise note taking, e.g.
Use a highlighter or underline key words or essential points in a passage.
Extract and list points.
- Demonstrate and practise diagrammatic ways of showing information.
- Delete excess words from a prepared passage to retain basic meaning.
- Rewrite passages as messages, headlines, telegrams, fifty word sagas.
- Contract long sentences, e.g.

> The Princess stared fixedly into the glowing embers of the dying fire. She was lost in a world of her own, drifting on the edge of sleep.

becomes

> The Princess stared into the fire dreamily, almost asleep.

- Embed sentences, where possible, from a list of paired sentences, e.g.

> Tom dived into the lake to save the girl. He did not have a thought for his own safety.

could become

> Tom, without thinking of himself, dived into the lake to save the girl.

- Write brief summaries in non-fiction, pretending to be reporters who have only been given one half of a column space.

Use:

Bullet points.
Numbered lists.
Flow charts.
Colums.
Headings.
Tables.

Relevant published materials/resources

NLS Activity Resource Sheet

Year	5
Term	2
Strand	S 10

Objectives

To ensure that, in using pronouns, it is clear to what or to whom they refer.

Activities

Shared or Group activity

- Use cloze procedure to delete pronouns.
- List and categorise under headings, e.g.

> Personal (I),
> possessive (mine),
> question (who),
> relative (theirs).

- Revisit work on collective nouns and proper nouns (Year 4 Term 2 S9).
- Distinguish between concrete nouns and abstractive nouns (thoughts, feelings and ideas).
- Reorganise a given list of nouns under headings in a grid. See diagram opposite.
- On a prepared passage children take out all the pronouns and insert nouns or vice versa – does it sound ridiculous? e.g. *'Bill Smith said to Bill Smith's mother that Bill Smith wanted a new bike for Bill Smith'.*

Collective	Proper	Abstract
library flock	Ranjit Bexley	a wish an idea

- From a list of sentences about a character create a narrative by substituting pronouns.
- Proof-read a prepared passage (and each other's writing) for verb/ subject agreement – number, person and tense.
- Give children prepared passages with errors of agreement for them to check, e.g. shift from *I* to *she*.
- When marking pro-actively ask children to check for specific details of agreement where errors have occurred, e.g. *'You started writing in the first person but there are three places where you have moved to third person – can you find them?'*

Relevant published materials/resources

NLS Activity Resource Sheet

Objectives

To read a range of explanatory texts, investigating and noting features of impersonal style, e.g. complex sentences: use of passive voice; technical vocabulary; hypothetical language (*if ... then*, *might*, *when the* ...); use of words/phrases to make sequential, causal, logical connections, e.g. *while, during, after, because, due to, only when, so*.

Activities

Shared or Group activity

- Extract, especially from exposition, connecting words or phrases that are used to help argue a point or persuade. List these, e.g.

> while, unless, although, whereas, because, since, in order to, so that, as if, moreover, it is clear that, consequently, therefore, so you see, however, nevertheless, etc.

- Practise using such connectives by completing simple stems, selecting an appropriate connective, e.g. *smoking is bad* becomes *smoking is bad since nicotine is poisonous,* etc.
- Purposefully use these terms while constructing persuasive writing. Demonstrate before children use the list, to help write powerfully and persuasively. Construct the overarching structure for an exposition. Introduce argument, cite a solution, provide reasons, cite possible objections, give overriding reasons, conclude. Use connecting words in sentences to act as a writing frame.

Relevant published materials/resources

NLS Activity Resource Sheet

Year	5
Term	3
Strand	S 3

Objectives

To search for, identify and classify a range of prepositions: *back*, *up*, *down*, *across*, *through*, *on*, etc.; experiment with substituting different prepositions and their effect on meaning. Understand and use the term 'preposition'.

Activities

Shared and Group Reading

- Identify prepositions as words that indicate the position of a noun within a sentence.
- Use prepositions in gymnastics, e.g. *run forwards, backwards, etc.*
- Write a preposition list poem, e.g.

> Above the sky, eternity lurks.
> Above the roof, the chimney squats.
> Above the scalp, hairs bristle ..., etc.

- Prepare cloze procedure with prepositions extracted.
- Produce passages with prepositions muddled up.
- Use colour-coded words to reinforce the function and place in sentences of prepositions.

Relevant published materials/resources

NLS Activity Resource Sheet

Year	5
Term	3
Strand	S 4

Objectives

To use punctuation marks accurately in complex sentences.

Activities

Shared and Group activity

- Investigate in groups how commas are used in a given passage or own reading books. Prepare a poster or presentation for the plenary defining three different times when a comma might be used. Provide examples to illustrate.
- Read sentences, then passages with no commas. Insert where they should be.
- Reinforce use of commas during Shared Writing – to break up a list, give a pause in a sentence, 'bracket' extra information that is dropped into a sentence, e.g. *Sally, who knew no fear, faced the lion.*
- List words or places in sentences which usually are followed by a comma, e.g. *however, meanwhile, certainly, inevitably, cautiously, later on, ... etc.*

> Before she/he said, e.g. "Come on," she said.
> After he/she said, e.g. She said, "come on."

- Find examples of longer, more complex sentences that use a comma e.g. *Staring helplessly at the branch, they began to crawl towards the tree trunk. Burglars, especially those who are dangerous, must be treated with caution,* etc.
- Notice, discuss and draw attention to the use of commas in reading.
- Use proof-reading as a taught, group activity to discuss instances using a passage with little, no or incorrect punctuation.
- Devise cloze procedures where punctuation marks have been replaced by other symbols. Ask children to list and try to decide which are commas, etc.

Relevant published materials/resources

NLS Activity Resource Sheet

Objectives

To investigate clauses through: identifying the main clause in a long sentence; investigating sentences which contain more than one clause; understanding how clauses are connected (e.g. by combining three short sentences into one).

Activities

Shared and Group activity

- Identify and list simple sentences, e.g. *I saw a dog. The dog ran by the shed,* etc.
- Identify and list complex sentences, e.g. *I made an omelet and I boiled up a cup of tea ...*
When I had made an omelet I boiled up a cup of tea because I needed to quench my thirst.
- Use coloured markers to show how complex sentences consist of different clauses joined together. Highlight clauses in one colour and the words used to connect in another colour. Each clause will contain a verb, e.g. *I **made** an omelet and I **boiled** up a cup of tea.*
- Examine complex sentences to see if you can 'extract' simple sentences, e.g.

> Although the wood cutter was strong it soon became evident that his axe was worse than useless.
> **becomes**
> The wood cutter was strong. His axe was useless.

- Extract phrases (groups of words with no verb) from complex sentences, e.g.

> Cindy wandered down to the noisy arcade so that she could buy a fluffy dog.
>
> **Phrases:**
> the noisy arcade, a fluffy dog.

Relevant published materials/resources

NLS Activity Resource Sheet

Objectives

To use connectives to link clauses within sentences and to link sentences in longer texts.

Activities

Shared or Group Writing

● List simple phrases, clauses and sentences onto cards as well as connecting words, e.g. *although, because, nevertheless, if after, however, since, therefore, during, until, when, etc.*

● Combine sentences, clause and phrases using connectives to make complex sentences, e.g.

---

phrases – her fluffy dog, the poodle parlour, a bad cold, etc.
clauses and sentences – Joanna went slowly down the road, it had, etc.

Becomes

Joanna went slowly down the road **with** her fluffy dog **towards** the poodle parlour **because** it had a bad cold.
(Connectives in bold.)

● If you present a reasonably long list some amusing and possibly bizarre sentences can be invented!

● Play a variation of the parlour game 'consequences'. In threes, one child lists simple sentences or clauses into a first column. The next child lists possible connectives. The third lists more simple sentences. When the paper is unfolded interesting combinations emerge, e.g.

I saw a peacock
although
the dog was barking.

● 'Drop' clauses or phrases into simple sentences to extend or add detail, e.g.
'The train that Jane had taken was late.'

Relevant published materials/resources

© Crown copyright 1998

NLS Activity Resource Sheet

Year	5
Term	3
Strand	T 15

Objectives

From reading to collect and investigate use of persuasive devices, e.g. words and phrases, e.g. 'surely', 'it wouldn't be very difficult ...'; persuasive definitions e.g. 'no one but a complete idiot ...'; rhetorical questions 'are we expected to ...', 'where will future audience come from ...?'; pandering condescension, concession, etc.; 'Naturally, it takes time for local residents ...' deliberate ambiguities.

Activities

Shared and Group Reading

- From a range of persuasive texts play 'spot the bias'. Underline whenever the writer is trying to persuade the reader. Circle the specific words used. Extract and list these in a chart.
- Imitate the language of persuasion through studying adverts and extracting persuasive phrases and clauses.
- Create adverts to sell off the class hamster, Henry VIII, a friend, etc.
- Create a collage of advertising phrases cut from magazines.
- In longer articles read and highlight persuasive language. Report back listing the instances. Explain the viewpoint that the article is persuading the reader to and the opposite view.
- Model the use of persuasive phrases in Shared Writing; link to non-fiction work.
- Practise using persuasive phrases by writing short, expository texts, purposefully using different devices.

> To persuade readers use the following ...

Relevant published materials/resources

© Crown copyright 1998

NLS Activity Resource Sheet

Year	6
Term	1
Strand	S 2

Objectives

To revise earlier work on verbs and to understand the terms *active* and *passive*; being able to transform a sentence from active to passive and vice versa.

Activities

Shared or Group activity

- Write active and passive sentences onto strips of paper/card. Children sort these into active/passive. They select one of each and imitate.
- Find and list three sentences in active voice.
- Transform into passive voice by swapping the subject round.
- Find and list three sentences in passive voice. Transform into active voice.
- Reading a prepared passage to revise. Identify verbs in passive voice, transform into active voice.
- Discuss with class the emphasis and focus in such sentences: *The boy was buying a banana; The banana is bought by the boy.* Does the writer intend the focus to be on what the boy is doing, or should the focus be on the banana?

N.B.
A verb is 'active' when the subject in a sentence performs the action, e.g. 'Boy buys banana'. To turn the verb into passive voice the banana becomes the subject and an auxiliary verb is needed e.g. 'Banana is bought by boy'. Most writing favours an active voice as being simple, direct and clear.

Relevant published materials/resources

NLS Activity Resource Sheet

Objectives

To investigate connecting words and phrases.

Activities

Shared or Group Reading

- Search different texts and list connectives. Do certain connectives appear mainly in certain text types? e.g. are there some connectives that are essential for expositions?
- Categorise connectives under suggested headings: location, position, number, order, time, comparison, argument, deduction, explanation, condition (if, unless), contrast (whereas, while).
- Groups feedback on these lists, showing different categories on a grid. For each category give some examples of sentences. Some connectives may appear in several columns.
- Play 'Boring Sentences'. Children invent short dull sentences, e.g. *The worm went.*
- List these and then use connectives to see who can transform them into the most interesting sentence, e.g.
The slim worm wriggled into a pair of trousers because his Bermuda shorts were at the cleaners.
- Using cloze procedure, omit connectives so that the children have to predict which connective is needed from their reading of the rest of the sentence.

Connective collection

Location/position: beside, nearby, under, far away ...
Number/order: first, second, then, next ...
Time: just, then, while, as, before ...
Comparison: by the same token, similarly, like, on the other hand ...
Argument/deduction: thus, therefore, while, whereas, only, when, as long as ...
Explanation: because, when, if ... then, by ...
Condition: if, unless ...
Contrast: whereas, while ...

Relevant published materials/resources

© Crown copyright 1998

NLS Activity Resource Sheet

Objectives

To form complex sentences.

Activities

Shared or Group activity
- As a class, revisit basic types of sentences, by sorting a list into types (statement, order, question, exclamation) or using four colours to underline sentences in a passage, categorising each one.
- Inventing examples of each sentence type, related to an example of each that might be spoken by a teacher, a parent, an alien, etc.
- Join examples of simple sentences with 'and', e.g. *Sally was walking. She saw a dog* becomes: *Sally was walking and she saw a dog.*
- Practise using connectives in different sentences, e.g.*Sally was walking because she missed the bus.* Then use the same connective to start the sentence
- Combine sentences using connectives, drop extra clauses into sentences, e.g. *Sally, her heart beating madly, was walking because she had missed the bus.*
Or ... *Sally was walking, even though it was late, because she had missed the bus.*
- Find examples from reading of sentences with extra clauses dropped into them. Imitate their structure, e.g. *The lorry thundered down the road, tyres spinning, till it came to a halt* can be imitated as, *The parrot flew over the jungle, wings flapping, while the hunter tied a shoelace.*
- Turn such complex sentences back into two or three simpler ones. *The parrot flew over the jungle. The parrot's wings flapped. Meanwhile, the hunter tied a shoelace.* Decide which sounds most effective.
- Provide a range of simple sentences and connectives on strips of paper. Let children experiment with combining and creating sentences. Who can make the longest, whilst retaining meaning? Create different types of sentences – a line from a play, a poem, a story, an explanation, an advert, etc.

Relevant published materials/resources

NLS Activity Resource Sheet

Objectives

To form complex sentences through using different connecting devices.

Activities

Shared or Group Writing

● Collect and list a broad range of connectives, including more 'demanding' words such as:

until, before, unless, although, if, whereas, previously, moreover, therefore, however, while, because, since, consequently, in order to, so that, as if.

● Children could experiment with simple sentences, using different connectives to see which ones work and what happens to the sentence, e.g.

> I woke early, before my alarm clock rang.
> I woke early, in case I missed the bus.
> I woke early, although I was really tired.

● Practise starting sentences with connectives, e.g. *Although I was really tired, I woke early*, etc. Categorise effects on the sentence. You may need to begin with a limited range of connectives, steadily adding more.

● Play 'Nursery Rhyme Game'. Children extend each line of a well known rhyme with a connective, e.g.

> *Mary had a little lamb, moreover she had two pigs as well. Its fleece was white as snow while its ears were brown. Everywhere that Mary went, although she wanted to be alone, the little lamb would go, since ...*

● Once children are practised at extending sentences with different connectives play the 'Fairy Tale Game'. To do this, have different connectives written on cards in a hat or dealt out to each child. In a circle, the children retell a well known story, e.g. 'The Three Little Pigs', but each sentence has to contain the connective that they have been dealt or that they pull from the hat, e.g.

> *Once upon a time there were three little pigs but they needed to leave home. Early one morning they said goodbye to their mother even though she was sad. Furthermore, they said goodbye to their friends ...*

● Play 'good news/bad news' using the opening clauses: *The good/bad news is that ... because ...*

Relevant published materials/resources

NLS Activity Resource Sheet

Objectives

To investigate further the use of the terms active and passive.

Activities

Shared or Group activity

● Revise notion of active and passive, turning sentences from active to passive or vice versa, e.g.

> Joanna drives a Ford Escort
>
> becomes
>
> A Ford Escort was being driven by Joanna.

● Indicate how the subject moves as the mood is changed, e.g.

> **Suzy** drew a picture.
> A picture was drawn by **Suzy**.

● Search for examples of passive voice, especially in non-fiction. List examples and transform into active voice. Compare and discuss effectiveness.
● Provide examples of sentences written in active and passive voices. Children compare and decide which communicates more powerfully.

Relevant published materials/resources

NLS Activity Resource Sheet

Objectives

To investigate further the use of the terms active and passive.

Activities

Shared or Group activity
- Use a list of examples of active/passive voice to underline which part of the sentence is being emphasised, e.g.

Passengers are asked to take their seats.

- Locate examples in different texts. Children should prepare a presentation for a plenary to explain why examples are in passive and not in active voice.
- Consider the purpose of such texts and the effect of using passive voice.
- Consciously use the terminology and encourage children to do so.
Imitate passages from reading.

Relevant published materials/resources

© Crown copyright 1998

NLS Activity Resource Sheet

Objectives

To revise work on complex sentences.

Activities

Shared and Group activity

● Circle in one colour 'subject' in simple sentence, 'verb' in another colour and 'object' in a third colour. On strips of paper write simple sentences. Colour in the subject, verb and object. Then swop them round to create different and strange combinations, e.g.

> **Dog bites man**
>
> becomes
>
> **Man bites dog.**

● On strips of paper move simple sentences around to create different compound sentences (joined by 'and' or 'but'). In a compound sentence both sections are dramatically equal, e.g. *I saw a dog and the dog ran away.*

● Introduce cards with more demanding connectives to add onto simple sentences. Complete by writing end clauses to finish the sentences.

● Cut up paragraphs into sentences. Children have to reassemble paragraph.

● Write short paragraphs of narrative, by extending an invented complex sentence from above activities.

Relevant published materials/resources

© Crown copyright 1998

NLS Activity Resource Sheet

Year	6
Term	2
Strand	S 3

Objectives

To revise work on complex sentences.

N.B.
In a complex sentence there will be a main clause which tells the reader the main/most important thing/aspect. Subordinate clauses are any other clauses in that sentence.

Activities

Shared activity

● From a complex sentence circle, highlight or underline the main clause. This will be the main thing that happens in the sentence. Usually it will be able to stand on its own. Teach children to apply this test, e.g.

> During the night I slept soundly despite a terrible storm.
>
> During the night – does not stand alone.
> I slept soundly – does stand alone. Main clause
> Despite a terrible storm – does not stand alone.

Group activity

● Provide a number of main and subordinate clauses on cards/paper. Children move these around to create complete sentences in different combinations.

Relevant published materials/resources

© Crown copyright 1998

NLS Activity Resource Sheet

Objectives

To revise work on contracting sentences.

Activities

Shared or Group activity

● Use a few complex sentences and show how they can be contracted by taking out detail, making them into simple sentences or reducing them to a few key words.

● Demonstrate how notes can be taken from a passage by using a highlighter to extract key words or phrases. Let the children delete words and phrases that are not necessary, listing the main points.

● Change writing that explains sequences or instructions to simple flow charts, e.g. *life cycle, rain cycle, recipe, rules for a game.*

● Extract a given number of bullet points from a text. Or ask the children to extract the five most important points.

● Edit each other's own note-taking and summarise to ensure brevity whilst capturing the main points.

● Edit a prepared example of note taking that contains a ridiculous amount of lengthy material that is not needed, e.g.

> The chapter starts off telling us that the Greens really liked to sit around listening to stories being told.

becomes:

> Chapter begins – Greens liked storytelling.

Relevant published materials/resources

NLS Activity Resource Sheet

Year	6
Term	2
Strand	S 4

Objectives

To revise work on contracting sentences: summary, notemaking, editing.

Activities

Shared or Group activity

● List a set of complex sentences in a column. Children have to circle the key point and beside the sentence, in a second column, note the points, e.g.

Initial sentence	Key point
It has been discovered that the (Romans) were not adverse to serving up to their (guests) stuffed (dormice,) etc.	Romans served guests stuffed dormice, etc.

● Extract key points from news items, reports, etc. In pairs agree on final list. Use bullet points, alphabet or numbers to organise notes.

Relevant published materials/resources

© Crown copyright 1998

NLS Activity Resource Sheet

Year	6
Term	2
Strand	T 17

Objectives

To read and understand examples of official language and its characteristic features, e.g. through discussing consumer information, legal documents, layouts, use of footnotes, instructions, parentheses, headings, appendices and asterisks.

Activities

Shared or Group activity

● Provide examples of official language to read and analyse. Identify, extract and list typical words, phrases and expressions. Use these to write imitative sentences or passages. For example, use **The Jolly Postman** as a source to write official letters, e.g. an invitation from the King inviting the frog to a ball, a solicitor's letter from the three pigs to the wolf, formal reply to the King, etc.

● Read prepared examples of official language, e.g. a letter from a palace official about the arrangements in**Cinderella** for the ball.

● Children should read, identify places where style is inappropriate and revise, e.g.

> To whom it may concern.
> The Royal ball is to be held on the 20th of this month. Those wishing to attend should ensure that they are appropriately dressed. Carriages will be parked at the rear of the stables. Slap on your best gear and get your knees up for a range of dances.

● Children reply to the letter in an appropriate style.

Relevant published materials/resources

NLS Activity Resource Sheet

Year	6
Term	3
Strand	S 1

Objectives

To revise the language conventions and grammatical features of the different types of text such as: narrative, recounts, instructional texts, reports, explanatory texts, persuasive texts, discursive texts.

Activities

Shared or Group Reading

- Children analyse, from a sample, the structure of a text type, creating a framework. Report back at plenary describing the structure.
- Annotate a sample of text type to indicate examples of language features, e.g. *paragraph, punctuation, tense, person, dialogue, active verbs, adjectives, rhyme, adverbs, figurative language.* How many grammatical features can the children spot?
- Categorise different types of writing.
- Categorise different types of story, e.g. *fable, parable, legend, science fiction, domestic.*
- Add terms and information to a class glossary.
- Create a wall chart to label types of writing, e.g.

Type	Purpose	Audience	Structure	Features
fable	to make a moral point	children	opening two characters setting dilemma events ending	paragraphs, etc.

Relevant published materials/resources

NLS Activity Resource Sheet

Objectives

To revise the language conventions and grammatical features of the different kinds of texts.

Activities

Shared or Group Reading
- Children analyse from samples the structure of explanatory and persuasive writing, creating a framework. Report back at plenary describing structure.
- Annotate samples to indicate examples of grammatical features, e.g. *tense, voice, connectives, person, use of conditionals.*
- Categorise and list different types of explanatory and persuasive writing (advert, argument, viewpoints, etc.).
- Create a wall chart showing label, purpose, structure and grammatical features.
- Add terms and information to class glossary.

Relevant published materials/resources

NLS Activity Resource Sheet

Objectives

To revise the language conventions and grammatical features of the different kinds of texts.

Activities

Shared or Group Reading

- Children analyse samples to extract the structure of recounts, procedures and informational writing, creating frameworks. Report back at Plenary describing the structure.
- Annotate samples to indicate examples of grammatical features, e.g. *tense, person, chronological ordering, headings.*
- Categorise and list different types of recounts, procedures and informational writing.
- Create a wall chart showing label, purpose, structure and grammatical features.
- Add terms and information to class glossary.

Relevant published materials/resources

© Crown copyright 1998

NLS Activity Resource Sheet

Year	6
Term	3
Strand	S 2

Objectives

To conduct detailed language investigations through interviews, research and reading.

Activities

Shared and Group activity

- Collect and list figures of speech from reading and own knowledge.
- Collect examples from other cultures by searching through literature set in other countries, e.g. any books by Betsy Byars for Americanisms.
- Collect examples from the past by looking in older classics, e.g. **The Secret Garden, Black Beauty**, etc.
- Use reference books such as **Brewers Dictionary of Phrase and Fable** to discover origins, meaning and related phrases.
- Categorise by type into a phrase poem, e.g.

> My best friend is cool as a cucumber,
> sweet as honey,
> large as life ...

- Add to the list by inventing new phrases.
- Categorise by common subject, e.g. *The fat is in the fire, no smoke without fire, to play with fire, etc.*
- Write stories to explain proverbs' origins, e.g. *a bird in the hand is worth two in the bush.*
- Purposefully use figures of speech when writing stories to help make dialogue realistic.

Relevant published materials/resources

Brewers Dictionary of Phrases and Fable (Cassell). **What's in a Word?** Pathways (Collins Educational).

NLS Activity Resource Sheet

Objectives

To revise formal styles of writing: the impersonal voice; the use of the passive; management of complex sentences.

Activities

Shared or Group activity

- Revise a prepared text with errors in standard English.
- Proof-read own and other children's work to check for standard English. Chart common errors which pupils make.
- Practise circling, underlining or highlighting key words or phrases to extract information.
- Delete words in sentences that are not essential, and leave key words.
- Use bullet points, letters or numbers to list points.
- Summarise passages by writing stories as 50-word mini sagas or as a 100-word news report.
- Reduce lengthy sentences and passages to essential points.
- Play 'Boring sentences' constructing complex sentences from single words, connectives or simple sentences.
- Take a well-known traditional tale or nursery rhyme and use connectives to extend sentences, e.g.

> Humpty Dumpty sat on a wall so that he was able to have a good view of the town. Humpty Dumpty had a big fall whereas his sister stayed quite safely on top of the wall …

- Use complex sentences to explain, justify, argue and reason.
- Adopt an impersonal style, using passive voice, formal language and complex sentences to write presentations, e.g. role play involving a construction company presenting reasons for building a new reservoir which will submerge half a village.
- Use and apply grammatical knowledge when reading and writing at text level.

Relevant published materials/resources

Word link

Join the verbs that are related to each other.

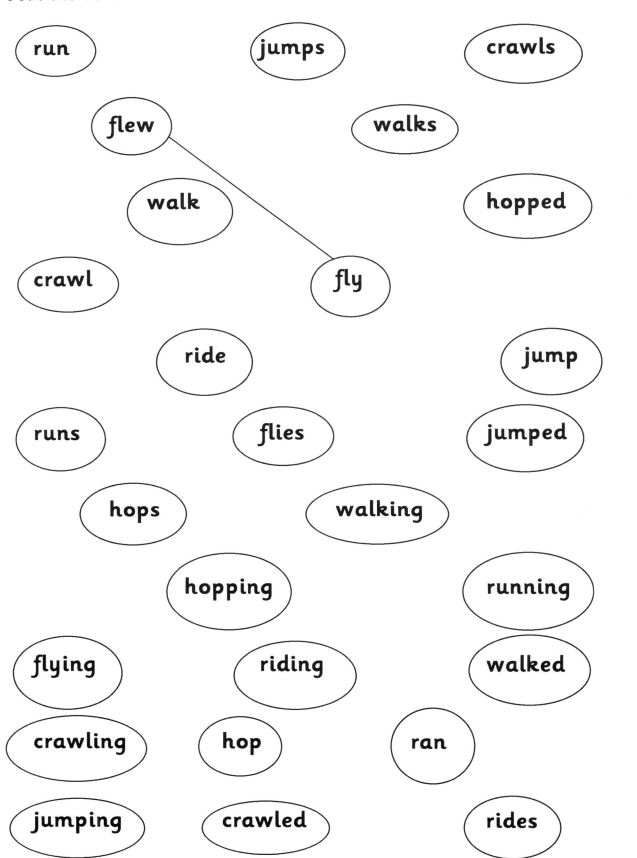

run   jumps   crawls

flew   walks

walk   hopped

crawl   fly

ride   jump

runs   flies   jumped

hops   walking

hopping   running

flying   riding   walked

crawling   hop   ran

jumping   crawled   rides

© Crown copyright 1998   Photocopiable Resource Sheet **Y3 T1 S 4**

Story beginnings games

Teacher information:

This game has been designed to develop knowledge about story openings in familiar texts.

- Demonstrate to the whole class.
- Children should then work independently in groups, especially if self-checking devices are included, i.e. original texts.
- The number of categories may vary.

You will need:

- a collection of story openings, collected over the week;
- a collection of book covers, or a collection of book titles;
- a collection of author names;
- a collection of story middle extracts or the next part of the story after the opening;
- a collection of story endings;
- a collection of characters.

Possible games:

- Match visually and give reasons.
- Turn over the items and pick up pairs.
- Turn over the items and collect a set (when all categories are used).
- Play a version of *Happy Families.*
- Play board games and collect various elements.

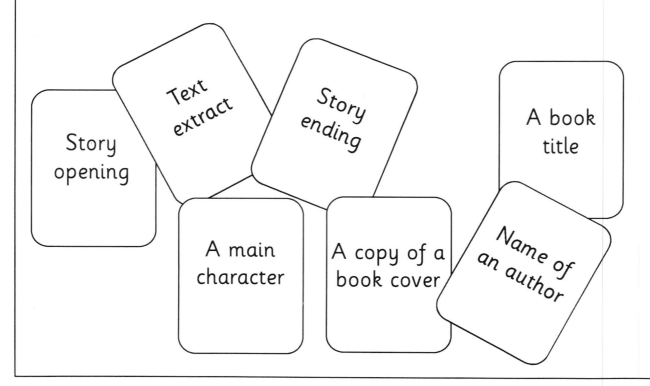

Make a sentence

I	like ice-cream.
You	can't do that.
The dogs	ate the bones.
Mr. Smith	is late for work.
We all	went to the zoo.
My mum	hates ironing.

© Crown copyright 1998

Two fish	swam in the sea.
He	caught the bus.
Those boys	are running fast.
Our car	is red.
Fatima	has new shoes.
They	are going home.
My sisters	look after me.

© Crown copyright 1998

Name:

Date:

Check it out! Persuasive writing

Persuasive writing	My comment	Teacher's comment
Does it say what the writing is about?		
Does the writer give reasons why certain actions should or should not be taken?		
How many reasons can you spot? Are these clear?		
Does it all make sense? Are there words which need to be changed?		
Do you feel persuaded?		
Other comment		

© Crown copyright 1998

Name:

Date:

Check it out! Procedural writing

Procedural writing	My comment	Teacher's comment
Are the instructions or directions easy to follow?		
Has the writer used the bullet points, or numbers or letters accurately?		
Has the writer left anything out?		
Try testing this out, if possible. Check spelling and punctuation.		
Other comments.		

© Crown copyright 1998

Name:
Date:

Check it out! Narrative

Narrative	My comment	Teacher's comment
Read the first paragraph. Does the beginning make sense? Is it clear?		
Does it have a good ending? Has anything been left out?		
Can you tell what is happening throughout the story? Why, or why not?		
Are there any words that need to be changed? If so, which?		
Is there any punctuation that needs to be changed? Is the spelling accurate?		
Other comments.		

© Crown copyright 1998

Name:

Date:

Check it out! Report

Report	My comment	Teacher's comment
Does it tell you what it is about at the start of the writing?		
Can you find four or more facts in the report? Is the writing clear?		
Is it written in the past tense? If not, why not?		
Does it have a clear meaning?		
Are there words or punctuation that need to be changed? If so, which? Is the spelling accurate?		
Other comments.		

© Crown copyright 1998

Name:

Date:

Standard and non-standard English

Non-standard spoken forms we use	Written standard English forms

© Crown copyright 1998